TRUST THE WILDNESS

A Trail Guide for Your Spiritual Journey

Lloyd Griffith

TRUST THE WILDNESS
A Trail Guide for Your Spiritual Journey

Copyright © 2013 Heart-Path Press
ISBN 978-0-578-11583-2

Heart-Path Press
232 Drake Landing
New Bern, NC 28560
(252) 675-8196

Cover Photo taken by Christopher Griffith
Cover Design by Meredith Griffith Heggland

To Cille

Anam Cara

ACKNOWLEDGEMENTS

The genesis for this trail guide came from a group of friends with whom I have spent over twenty years sailing coastal waters. The members of the Green Water Sailing Society observed my nightly journaling, leading to questions about the practice of contemplation. From these discussions, they developed an appreciation for the volume of journals I had accumulated over forty years. Their encouragement to tell the story preserved in these journals, before they were lost, persuaded me to undertake this project.

Revisiting these journals after three score and ten years, I have become acutely aware of companions who were sent at the right time to deliver me from myself, to reconnect me with things of the Spirit, and to encourage me to follow its leading. I owe sincere gratitude to all those angels for the new life they guided me to discover.

Unfortunately, time does not allow me to formally thank all those who deserve recognition, but please know the significance of your presence. I must, however, acknowledge some who consistently made significant interventions on my journey. The Reverend Dr. John Philip Newell clarified the Christian tradition's teaching on the presence of a holy kingdom. The Reverend Dr. Skip Johnson, companion for most of my journey, pried me loose from the world's tight grip that I might better recognize this kingdom. The Reverend Dr. William C. Bennett introduced me to an established reformed tradition that was still alive with the movement of the Spirit and helped me learn to refocus on its presence.

Charlie and Clayton Burns, Jim Epps, Dr. Roger Christian, Dr. Bob Bilbro, and Dr. Reed Underhill, were good friends who stood by me long enough to become the brothers I never had and helped me grow to respect my own heart. Rose Helms led me to listen to my heart and stand by its stirrings in the midst of trials and sufferings. Bob, Bo, Mike, and Reed, my sailing companions, taught me to trust my compass—the soul's light—when the way was uncertain.

My family has inspired and stood by me faithfully through this project. My adult children showed me much about the spiritual journey: Christopher's release of conventional wisdom to pursue his dream, and Meredith's alignment at her crossroad to another natural, heart-felt dimension of reality. The unhurried pace of Yao Amamoo, an African chieftain who adopted our family thirty years ago, revealed a trust in an ancient wildness in the midst of a frenzied, postmodern world.

Finally, Cille, my wife and partner, has shared most of this journey with me. I first recognized the spiritual *wildness* in her, and we have grown together in learning to find and follow its movement in our life together. She probably never considered herself a spiritual companion—most don't. But when I struggled to discern my way through confusion, she listened me back into clarity. When I held on to my head, she directed me to my heart. When I faced tough choices, she guided me beyond rigid adherence to old beliefs to trust a more spontaneous Spirit. When I retreated to the study, she respected my space for a while, but then called me back to others and life. Most important, when I could not love myself, she continued to love me. Her steadfast love is a faithful presence of something greater reaching out to me beyond my time.

She is and has always been my soul mate: *Anam Cara.*

Lloyd Griffith   06/15/2013

It was I who fed you in the wilderness.
Hosea 13:5 (NRSV)

Table of Contents

INTRODUCTION

The Kingdom of God at Hand

The Kingdom of God is not coming with things that can be observed; nor will they say, "Look, here it is!" or "There it is!"
For, in fact, the kingdom of God is among you.
Luke 17:20 – 21

Wake up!

This trail guide is an invitation to join me on a journey to find your *heart-path*—your way in a world that has the Sacred in it.

My interest and appreciation for this sacred dimension in life has grown from lifelong experiences with young people. I am not by profession a theologian, although I do have

1

seminary training and ordination in the Presbyterian Church (USA) and lay claim to being "theologian in residence" in my own life. To that foundation, I've added a master's degree in counseling psychology and a certificate in spiritual formation. But it was my years as a professional in resident camping that awakened me to the presence and power of another, deeper dimension in life.

The young people I came to know through camping brought a fresh, mostly uncluttered perspective to life. They shared the innocence of being "in but not yet of"—not fully invested in—the world. As they ventured out into that world, some caught a glimpse of something *more*—an inner presence, a "still, small voice within," longing to be heard. They became aware of another dimension of reality beyond the more familiar material world of sights and sounds. This inward

INTRODUCTION

spiritual reality held hopes, dreams, and aspirations that transcended their everyday lives.

Others, not so lucky, took longer to wake up to this soulfulness—this awareness of something more spiritual. I was in that group, narrowly focused on managing the demands of the material world. I was sleepwalking through my days, missing invitations to a more abundant life.

This is the story of my waking up. It is a story of learning, in spite of living in our postmodern, technocentric world where we so often find ourselves disconnected from things of the Spirit, to trust in the spiritual wildness that will lead us to the Sacred that surrounds us.

Finding Our Way

Different religions provide "maps"—stories, rituals, and practices—to provide direction to the sacred dimension and allow the faithful to experience it. But, like all maps, they are human creations. Differences among them reflect variances in the particular cultures and times in which they came into being. The map is not the reality; it is a representation that helps us understand that reality and find our way to it. It is not the Sacred; it is a guide for getting to and living in relationship with the Sacred.

The Christian tradition has been my map into this spiritual territory. It is the legacy into which I was born and in which I still feel most at home. Because of its comfortable familiarity, this tradition became the vehicle by which the wisdom of the Holy was mediated to me, witnessing to a kingdom of God close at hand and teaching me a way to it.

In my tradition, Jesus Christ is the mediator between the material and spiritual dimensions. He taught and modeled a way to the Spirit that was rooted in the contemplative practices of loving God with one's whole being and one's neighbor as oneself (Mark 12:29–31).

Fundamentalists and modernists now debate the interpretation of this tradition. I grew up in a church that accepted the biblical story as literally true, a perspective challenged by a modern, scientific culture that dismisses anything that reason can't explain as mere fiction.

This guide relates how I learned to move beyond both of those points of view using contemplative practices to encounter the Spirit of God, which I found increasingly real and true. By following Jesus' way I became more contemplative in my actions, making room for my soul—an eternal element that "magnifies the Lord" (Luke 2:46). Walking this path revealed unearthly possibilities in ordinary life—the spiritual kingdom Jesus assured his followers was close at hand, but unlike any kingdom they had ever known.

Skills for the Journey

I made my way to this spiritual kingdom along a path of contemplation, one I had unconsciously begun to follow years before in summer camp, where I regularly left behind the habits and expectations of my normal routine. Clothing myself in the traditional Christian virtues of faith, hope, and love, I learned to pay attention to signs, intuitions, and calls of the Spirit.

Releasing my habitual attempts to control the outcomes of my behavior, I put on faith in the Spirit, freeing my mind from conventional wisdom. Refocusing on moments of inspirations in nightly devotions and Sunday services, I put on hope in the Spirit present in all life. Responding to infusions of the soul's light that altered my

INTRODUCTION

consciousness, I put on love for the Spirit, following it in my choices. Trusting this *wildness*—this movement of the Spirit—I found a way to my heart-path, the place where the Holy was active in my life. A holy vision was joined with a sacred calling at a particular time and place, putting love into action. It was my way in this spiritual kingdom.

A Pilgrim's Progress

I found my way in this spiritual kingdom by learning to trust the wildness. Traces of Its presence are preserved in my collection of journals kept over the past forty years. These journals have been a rich resource for recalling the chronology and details of my journey. But the events themselves are only the beginning; the real story is the spiritual presence I discovered reaching out to me through those events.

TRUST THE WILDNESS

Returning to these journals at this juncture in my life, I wanted to reexamine these recorded experiences to determine whether and where holiness was present. My aim was to move beyond the events themselves to get at their meaning, a meaning I had often missed at the time.

In looking inward and gazing back along the trail I have journeyed, I have attempted to be faithful to the emotional truth of those experiences, which goes beyond the facts themselves. It filters those facts through my imagination as a way of recalling their meaning for me. Given my bent toward pleasing others, this personal, emotional dimension was both the most challenging and the most helpful part in writing this guide. Painful incidents and unresolved issues initially pleaded to be left undisturbed, blocking my way to the truth.

INTRODUCTION

Reading through these journals again, now in a more contemplative manner, ordinary events and encounters were transfigured, revealing the Holy reaching out to me, again and again, along my path. Recording daily activities, I became more contemplative, putting on faith, hope, and love to be more reflective of the Spirit's presence.

How to Use This Guide

I offer this record of my own journey in the hope that it can help you find your way in this kingdom. It is organized into five distinct passages, dimensions of spiritual consciousness that opened up as I grew in soulfulness, responding to the movement of the Spirit in my life. In each chapter, I describe memories or journal entries that reveal a spiritual crisis, the obstacles I encountered as I tried to overcome it, its eventual resolution, and the expansion of my consciousness of something *more* to which it led.

9

TRUST THE WILDNESS

Note that the resolution of a particular crisis in no way implies the end of the journey. The truth is that, like the wind, the Spirit moves and changes constantly. It is the task of a lifetime to discover and rediscover your heart-path—the place where the Holy is active in your life.

Like most trail guides, this one has a staccato style, composed of important guide notes and high points or dangers to notice on a portion of the trail. This rhythm misses the interludes of peace and joy that embellished my journey. Although it was often risky and demanding, a lot of really, really, really grace-filled moments came my way. I have been blessed with a freedom that bloomed beyond the limitations of conventional wisdom; with a peace that came in possessing my own life in alignment with something much greater than myself; and with a joy in finding my true way in a world that conspires to make everyone alike.

INTRODUCTION

Once your journey begins, you will start to live by faith in the soul's light stirring within all of us. You will pay more attention to signs, intuitions, and calls of the Spirit as you learn to trust the wildness. You will grow in soulfulness, in increased awareness of inspirations, visions, and heart-paths that renew your integrity and your understanding of who you are called to be *at this moment*.

Your journey, obviously, will differ from mine. Your road will present its own unique challenges. But you can employ the same skills to become more contemplative in your actions and to trust the wildness reaching out to you. Faith, hope, and love create a receptive attitude for the Spirit. Like a VHF emergency radio, they set your dial on receive, attending to the presence of something *more* and remaining alert to inspirations, visions, and heat-paths that reveal the kingdom of God.

TRUST THE WILDNESS

One skill I've learned is how to recognize the "thin places" that surrounded me at particular points in my life journey, and how to seek these out on my own rather than haphazardly falling into them now and then. I hope this guide will serve as a useful companion, offering you a way of being more intentional in finding those extraordinary places yourself.

It will be an adventure!

INTRODUCTION

Ponder

1. What was the point of departure for your spiritual journey? What happened to raise questions about the direction in which you were traveling?
2. What were some of the significant turning points along your way: closed doors, crossroads, or dark nights?
3. What was your call—your longing for something *more?*
4. What maps have you found helpful in understanding spiritual territory?
5. What is your destination? How far have you gone? What have you learned?

NOVICE

*But now you must get rid of all such things—
anger, wrath, malice, slander, and abusive
language from your mouth. Do not lie to one
another, seeing you have stripped off the old self
with its practices.* Colossians 3:8–9

Base Camp: Wadesboro, North Carolina. To speak of a journey assumes a starting point, a place or origination where one left home. It implies a departure from that which is known and familiar.

Clues to who I am today, my basic personality, my outlook on life, lie within my earliest memories of growing up. As an adult, I carry around a small, frightened child whose perception of the way things "should be" is bound to my early recollections of this world. Truthfully, I would have preferred to leave some of these old memories buried quietly in the past. But the only way to begin a spiritual journey in earnest is to uncover those assumptions and expectations in search of the hidden self.

I grew up in Wadesboro, a small agricultural and mill community sixty miles east of Charlotte. The neighborhood that formed the boundaries of my world teemed with children with whom I attended school (segregated at the time) and whose stay-at-home moms took responsibility for every youngster within range of their voices. Church membership was assumed. Most people I knew attended one of the four mainline Protestant churches.

"Father Knows Best," a popular TV comedy, colored my picture of what a family was supposed to be. In each episode Jim Anderson returned home from work, took off his hat, hung up his jacket, and within the show's half-hour format resolved whatever quandaries confronted his family. School, friendships, and relationships with the opposite sex were easily solved with a smile and a few words of sensible advice from Father.

<u>Memory, April, 1954:</u> Marker Moment. During school recess I joined several friends staring at a billowing black cloud rising in the western sky. Piecing together bits of the conversation, I realized the smoke was coming from my father's laundry business. A sick emptiness in the pit of my stomach replaced whatever I had just finished for lunch. As soon as school ended, I raced home, where my mother shared details of the disastrous fire: a tiny electric spark on cleaning solvent had set off an explosion. Only charred fragments of clothes and shells of scorched equipment remained. For me, the impact of the fire was conveyed by the defeat that replaced the joy I had known in my father's eyes.

1. **Guide Note: Contemplation.** Here I came to one of the key turning places in the trail. To go deeper, I put on faith in the Spirit, stripping off my old self, with its practices I had acquired from family and community, and opening my heart to something *more* in life.

Memory, Winter, 1954: Shifting Attention. The fire's effect on my family was devastating. As my father's efforts at recovery failed, my parents' world disintegrated into dependence on alcohol to ease their pain. As things went from bad to worse financially, their lives eroded into weekend binges and nightly shouting matches.

A small chapel at the Methodist Church became a safe haven from this oppressive atmosphere. I found my way to this haven when I was asked to usher for evening services regularly attended by a dozen or two members. This quiet space, with its family atmosphere of acceptance and security, immersed me in a practice of prayer, shifting my attention to a holy kingdom and offering me a respite from the chaos at home.

Memory, Spring, 1956: Detaching from the Familiar. A patrol car pulled up to our front door. I overheard the sheriff inform my mother of my father's arrest for drunk driving. My family's secret was exposed. My growing suspicion that *my* father didn't "know best" had been confirmed.

Memory, Fall, 1956: Freeing My Mind. I escaped the growing turmoil at home, learning to meet my needs for esteem and affection through athletics. For a teenager in my small town, athletics was one of the few paths to recognition and approval. I had seen older boys become sports stars, their accomplishments profiled in the local newspapers. Athletic success became my obsession. I devoted all my free time to rigorous practice to ensure it.

My back yard was bordered by a garage, a fence, and a swing set that created an outdoor arena for a basketball goal. It was the site of intense imaginary games in which, time after time, I sank the final shot to clinch the championship.

Memory, Spring, 1959: Resisting Change. I was bound on my quest for success when I tried out for the football team at Duke University. While most of the freshmen had been recruited, I "walked on," hoping to earn a place on the team. After a discouraging week of practice, I found myself relegated to a low position on the roster.

TRUST THE WILDNESS

For the first time ever, self-doubts broke through the façade of my acquired wisdom. Discouraged and frightened, I impulsively quit the team.

A torrent of guilt doused my temporary sense of relief in leaving the football team. I had let myself down. From junior high school on, football had been my ticket to self-esteem. I kicked myself for quitting so soon.

I tried to rectify matters by going out for basketball, a turn in the road that came to a dead end when I didn't make the final cut. Desperate to avoid rejection, I reverted to football, devoting January and February to preparations for spring practice. I frantically clung to my belief in this well-worn path.

But in spite of a rigorous weight-training program and stuffing myself at meals, I was still only 175 pounds when practice started. Disillusioned by bruises, aches, and failure, I finally realized the

truth: I was too small for football. Habits I had
cultivated to protect my self-esteem were no
longer working. My best efforts would never
overcome the limitations of my size. In spite of—
or maybe because of—being flooded with dismay,
I woke up to signs that this was not the right path
for me. At the conclusion of spring practice, I
relinquished my assumed destiny as a football
star, turning aside from my contrived path to
praise and glory. I realized that my own
resources, while gifts, could not take me all the
way out of the disorder. Ultimately, I needed
spiritual resources beyond myself.

Memory, Spring, 1961: **Leaving Home.** I let go
of my acquired self, releasing my attempts to
control the outcome and making room for the
infusion of the Spirit. From the Methodist Church
in which I'd grown up, I had inherited an image of
a supernatural, judgmental God, separated from
creation. From time to time this super figure

intervened in life, rewarding "right" beliefs and "good" behavior and punishing "false" beliefs and "bad" behavior.

A class on religion and western literature at Duke University introduced me to a new image of God as a holy presence within life. My readings of pre-Christian biblical texts showed me a new, personal, perspective of a transcendent God who was powerfully invested in the created world, not separated from it. The classic Christian writers who followed—Dante, Milton, and Bunyan— revised this narrative of immanence from the New Testament perspective of the life and death of Jesus Christ. The full nature of this creator God was incarnated in the life and teachings of Jesus. Post-Christian writers of the twentieth century— T.S. Eliot, H. Richard Niebuhr, and Paul Tillich— witnessed to this same divine presence, with signs of continued infusions of a living God in the midst of false cultural idols.

My growing appreciation for the presence of something more in life led me beyond my earlier concerns with worldly success. This new vision of a creative spiritual energy flowing through ordinary life seemed truer and more present than the conventional wisdom I had acquired, allowing me to relax my tight grip on my earlier self-image.

Memory, Spring, 1962: **Opening My Heart.** As I began to let go of control, I awakened to "holy intrusions" in my life, intuitive impulses that seemed to beckon me. I was led back to a girl who had ended our earlier relationship when her idea of an exciting evening didn't include the college library. Cille's energetic, outside-the-box attitude nourished my emerging openness to the stirrings of the Spirit. Our relationship incited an untamed passion in me, resonating with something deep and true. Its authenticity was inviting, its wildness beyond my control, purifying my heart of its earlier prejudices. I was inspired by something larger than emotions, something beyond the range of my senses that would not be denied.

Memory, June 15, 1963: Becoming a Novice. Cille and I were married. Stripping off my old self and its practices, I was aware of the mystery of something more stirring in my life. I turned aside from my acquired wisdom, freeing my mind to pay more attention to a spiritual presence. I had become a novice on the spiritual journey.

But as a novice I continued to wander in and out of spiritual territory. My desire to control my own destiny made me resistant to moments of inspiration. I was anxious for approval and devoted to the idea that success was the way to ensure it. My inherited assumptions and conventional beliefs still blocked my awareness of the spiritual presence reaching out to me.

NOVICE

Ponder
1. What "home" of habits, expectations, and responsibilities do you bring from childhood?
2. What ways have you learned to defend against the chaos in life?
3. What longings draw you forward?
4. What signs do you perceive?
5. What new directions are you being invited to consider?

EXPLORER

Set your minds on things that are above, not on things that are on earth.
Colossians 3:2

Base Camp: Emory University. In the fall of 1965, following my graduation from Duke Divinity School, Cille and I moved to Atlanta, Georgia, where I started a PhD program in theology and literature at Emory University. This academic trail was well marked with courses to complete and papers to present. The doctorate was the final step in my career plan to teach religion and coach in a small college, neatly fusing my growing interest in life's spiritual dimension with my familiar zeal for athletics.

EXPLORER

Memory, January, 1966: **Marker Moment.** My faculty advisor recommended postponing my academic program to give me time to strengthen my background in literature. His comments fell like a sledgehammer, shattering my carefully constructed plans and opening new cracks in my self-perception. My mind raced back to the memory of failing to making the football team at Duke. Reeling from shock, I was forced to release my old assumptions about myself and my expectations for the future and let go of my mission to attain a PhD.

1. **Guide Note: Contemplation.** As I turned in faith toward the Spirit in this crisis, I began to relinquish my carefully crafted career plans, to leave my familiar home of acquired longings and expectations and begin my inner journey in earnest.

TRUST THE WILDNESS

Memory, February, 1966: **Shifting Attention.** In the space forced open by the professor's suggestions, I caught a whisper of the Spirit's intentions in Cille's tenacious confidence in me. This was nothing new; her positive thoughts had been part of my landscape all along. I just hadn't been paying attention. My focus on my own plans had built a wall her words could not penetrate. Now that wall was crumbling under the impact of failure and disappointment. I began to shift my attention to what she was telling me.

Memory, February, 1966: **Detaching from the Familiar.** My advisor's suggestion that I teach in a prep school while beefing up my strength in literature lingered with me and ignited memories of a colleague with whom I had worked at a YMCA camp the previous summer. He spent his winters teaching at Randolph Macon Academy in Front Royal, Virginia, and during our summer together he had spun intriguing yarns of his boarding school adventures. His tantalizing tales of school life resurfaced during this crisis, and, now that I was no longer so narrowly focused, allowed me to entertain the idea of trying a different direction.

<u>Memory, April, 1966:</u> Freeing My Mind. I researched faculty openings at a number of prep schools and submitted my résumé to three. I was especially attracted to The Asheville School, a small private male boarding school in the mountains of western North Carolina. The school served two hundred students in grades eight through twelve in a rigorous academic program based on a traditional core curriculum. I felt drawn by its mission to nurture the growth of the mind, body, and spirit of each student—exactly the kind of task I'd found so fulfilling in my job as a camp counselor. Excited by the prospect of working with young people again, I eagerly accepted their offer to join the faculty.

TRUST THE WILDNESS

<u>Memory, March, 1967:</u> Resisting Change. My initial excitement for this path soon wilted in the routine of classroom preparations and my frustrations as an ambitious assistant coach. I bounced between highs of engaging interactions with students, athletes, and faculty and lows of classroom apathy and meager athletic opportunities. My free time was consumed with supervising a dozen or more adolescents in the dorm.

Gradually, fatigue and disillusionment drained away the spiritual energy that had fueled this move. I'd already abandoned my dreams of a PhD; now I found myself questioning the goal of teaching and coaching. Staring at the tattered fragments of my career map, I had a gnawing sense of being exiled in some parched land. The map I had drawn for myself could take me no further.

EXPLORER

Memory, March, 1967: **Leaving Home.** I was intrigued by stories from several faculty members about their summer experiences at Camp Sequoyah, a boy's camp west of Asheville. Their enthusiastic memories renewed an interest in resident camping that drew me beyond my career in education.

Memory, April, 1967: **Opening My Heart.** I drove out to the camp in Weaverville, a short distance from the school. My first impressions were disappointing. Dead limbs rested on abandoned cabins; spider webs cloaked the doors. The desolate scene matched my despondency. Yet the warmth of the sun and exuberance of the wildflowers bordering the fresh green grass hinted at life's return.

After traipsing around the lake, cabins, and dining hall, I reached an open-air chapel nestled in the trees at the top of a hill. The peace and quiet of this sanctuary reminded me of the chapel in the Methodist Church of my childhood. In this natural setting, a dictum above the entrance welcomed me into that sacred space: "That they may value the Unseen and the Intangible—for of these Reality is fashioned." As my eyes adjusted to the intermingling of sunshine and shadows, they were drawn to the rafters, where quotations from campers and counselors extolled their own experience of the unseen and intangible. A fifteen-year-old's words spoke to the power of the place: "I really believe that was the first time I became aware of God."

Suddenly, I, too, became aware of a life-changing spiritual energy permeating the chapel. It was a powerful force, personally present in a way I had never experienced in academic pursuits. I couldn't articulate how I came to feel it; it just happened. The moment had not been planned. I was inspired by an intangible yet overwhelming feeling of something *more* suffusing that space.

This inspiration purged my heart of the discouragement in which it was drowning at school. For the first time since my engagement to Cille, my heart felt open again. I began to reconsider my plan to teach and to allow myself to think about another possibility: a career in residential camping.

Memory, June, 1967: Confronting Conflict.
Like a vivid dream that lingers into the morning, that openness stayed with me as I returned for my third summer at Camp Sea Gull. When I was invited to join the full-time staff, I was receptive, but continued to waver between giving up my ambitious plans for an academic career and following the alluring energy moving in a new direction.

TRUST THE WILDNESS

Two dark clouds cast shadows on my decision. The most obvious was the YMCA's entrenched practice of segregation. The year had been dominated by freedom marches, sit-ins, and race riots in the wake of the assassinations of President John Kennedy and Martin Luther King, Jr. I was drawn to the strong forces moving throughout the country for a more inclusive and just society. Yet in the South at that time, the YMCA, including the camp, found itself bound by deep-rooted cultural opposition to those forces.

Beyond that barrier was the camp director himself, a legend in the Y. His success had been built on the belief that excellence resides not in buildings, but in staff, and he brooked no compromise in his high expectations of his employees. For many of us growing up in his shadow, he was an inspiration. For me, he took the place of the father I lost to alcohol. Yet I sensed that his dominating style of leadership would, like a bulldozer, flatten any attempt I made to forge my own individual path.

2. **Guide Note: Meditation.** In the midst of this conflict, I put on hope in the Spirit. Journaling my actions and interactions changed my focus. Significant encounters with campers, colleagues, friends, and family began reappearing in daily entries, speaking for themselves, interrupting my obsession with managing my past and controlling my future. Their voices were faint at first, but, with repetition, they became increasingly forceful and clear, reinforcing some idea, feeling, or impulse.

   A moving passage in a book, the smile of a friend, even the sting of some disappointment became a minor ecstasy. My attention shifted from my head's search for success to my heart's intuitions. Such moments of inspiration transcended reason's reach, illumining my consciousness with direct insights beyond sight and sound.

Journal, July 5, 1967: Refocusing on the Spirit. In pondering my decision about camp, I was reading *New Perspectives for the YMCA* by Dr. Paul Limbert. The author offered a realistic evaluation of the substantial social changes the Civil Rights Movement had created in the urban communities the YMCA served. He thoughtfully outlined organizational and policy changes that could guide the institution in adapting its mission to the new social environment. This hopeful note of change refocused my attention beyond the organizational obstacles I was facing.

Journal, July 14, 1967: Respecting My Heart. My job as head counselor at the camp had involved planning and implementing an outdoor adventure program for 192 boys and 32 cabin leaders. My responsibilities were demanding, costly, often requiring a major sacrifice of personal time. Many were similar to responsibilities I'd shouldered at school, yet when I was honest with myself, I saw that their impact on me was much different. At school I had felt them as burdens, draining and dispiriting; at camp I had found them energizing. I'd felt freed, more available not only to the campers and other counselors, but to deep, authentic parts of my own life. Even in the most trying situations, in my heart, this work felt right.

Journal, August 17, 1967: Illumining the Path. Cille shed more light on my growing sense of the rightness of my pursuit of the camp idea. A soon-to-be mom, she was fully appreciative of the security a close-knit school community afforded. Having been both a camper and a counselor herself, however, she was enthusiastic about my taking the camp position. Clearly, she was ready, in spite of the trade-off, to make the move. Furthermore, Cille and I had both dreamed of her staying home with our baby for the first few years, and I wanted to do all I could to provide this opportunity for her. The salary at camp would go a long way toward making it a viable possibility.

I let go, finally, of the tattered remains of the career map to which I had been desperately clinging. In spite of lingering doubts about my abilities and the camp's openness to diversity, I perceived that camp was the right direction for me. I accepted the opportunity to serve as personnel director.

Journal, March 10, 1975: Coming to a Crossroad. My job involved recruiting, training, and supervising college and high school students to staff the summer camp program—an assignment encumbered by the social storm brewing at the time. Students across the country were protesting against the injustices of the Vietnam War and racial segregation. Authority, in general, had become suspect. Distrust tainted all institutions, even summer camps, deterring some idealistic young people from seeking employment with the YMCA.

I received an application from a highly qualified candidate I would have hired without question had he not been African American. During my early years in the job, I had been able to maneuver staff recruitment around the negatively charged storm of the Civil Rights Movement. This time was different.

Integration had become, by now, the official law of the land. The church I attended, following the lead of its social-prophet minister, championed the national move toward an integrated society. I was increasingly conscious of the massive injustice of the social segregation policies I had inherited. Nevertheless, powerful cultural forces resisted change. Those forces had a strong hold on the local business community and, consequently, the YMCA, which was dependent on community involvement for financial support. The camp, like most organizations in the South at the time, offered "separate but equal" services. The expected institutional response to this application was a referral to the "other" YMCA.

I agonized over my decision. Deferring this qualified applicant would, I felt, be morally wrong. Yet my worries about not following established employment practices choked my intuition, tempting me to turn back.

Journal, October 30, 1974: Persevering in the Spirit. The previous fall, at a career-development conference at Blue Ridge Assembly in Black

EXPLORER

Mountain, North Carolina, I'd experienced a major spiritual awakening. When my small group began to discuss organizational roles and relationships, I'd suddenly become strangely defensive, reluctant to delve into this area of my life. Fortunately (I was able to admit later), the group would not let me hide behind my cultivated Y persona. The persistent probing of my carefully created image of perfection eventually broke through my defenses. I blurted out my deep fear of rejection.

I felt vulnerable, exposed, stripped of my emotional camouflage. I retreated to the safety of an empty meeting room. As I shed, layer by hardened layer, my shell of perfection, a rush of long-exiled thoughts and feelings swept over me. I became conscious of deeper, inner places that my bondage to approval had obscured from sight. I saw my need to please binding me to the organization, even when it was in conflict with my own deeply held values. I began looking beyond easy accommodation to organizational or social expectations to refocus on the deeper movement of the Spirit.

Journal, March 18, 1975: **Finding a New Way.** An instructor in a parenting class guided me to "own" my growing appreciation for intuitions. The course incorporated skills in psychology and transactional analysis to help parents see their children as unique selves and, consequently, develop a different and more respectful relationship with them.

As my attitude shifted, I came to value my own uniqueness as well. Growing up, I had learned to set aside my thoughts and feelings trying to keep peace at home. The instructor, taking me by the hand with unconditional acceptance, steered me around my own internal interference back to the authenticity of my inner life. Getting beyond my habitual put-downs, I came to value, to truly appreciate, the intuitions resonating in my heart. It was then I recognized the truth: I could not allow the application from the African-American to die in the referral bin. I needed to proceed with it in spite of the obstacles. My consciousness had been altered by stirrings in my heart. At the time, I didn't think of this as a vision; my romantic notions of the concept precluded such a spiritual phenomenon within a mundane job conflict. However, I was learning that intuitions, while grounded in everyday circumstances, have a transcendent truth that goes beyond the events themselves.

Journal, April 8, 1975: **Becoming an Explorer.** Holding on to the pure stirrings in my heart rather than going along with conventional wisdom, I requested a meeting with the Y Board. Following my carefully crafted outline, I emphasized the Y's mission of character development; I reviewed the camp's long history of selecting outstanding staff to achieve that mission; and I concluded with a request to proceed with an application from an exceptionally well-qualified candidate who happened to be African-American.

Without comment, I was excused for an interminable moment while the board deliberated. When they were finished, I was told my request had been referred to the legal committee. I assumed the worst and waited for my supervisor to deliver the bad news.

It never came. The legal committee met the following week and approved my request. From a legal perspective, the response was a given. Employment laws had changed; it would have been illegal to rule otherwise. I woke up from a bad dream! My intuitions had been right and had navigated me around a monstrous obstacle.

EXPLORER

I had become an explorer on the spiritual journey. Refocusing, setting my mind on matters of the Spirit, and standing by my heart in spite of my ingrained ways of responding, a new and right spirit had been born in me. I grew in soulfulness; I was aware of the Spirit's longings in my own life. The dissonance that infected me at the beginning of this trail had been healed. I was aligned with the Spirit.

This new soulfulness did not conclude the spiritual journey. The shadow of self-doubt and my need to control still dogged me, often overriding my devotion to the Spirit. In times of testing, I fell back, trusting others more than the "still small voice" dwelling within, following my head at the expense of my heart. Learning to follow my heart led me on to Camp Becket, the next passage on my heart-path.

TRUST THE WILDNESS

Ponder

1. Where have you discovered "still waters"— the presence of the Spirit—in your life?
2. What obstacles block your spiritual path, leaving you confused and frustrated?
3. What practices help you refocus and pay attention to things of the Spirit?
4. Where do you feel yourself being drawn as you become more contemplative?
5. What revelation—your experience of the Holy—your privileged moment of truth— has been living in your imagination and suddenly is becoming part of your tangible world?

ADVENTURER

I had heard of you by the hearing of the ear, but now my eye sees you. Job 42:5

Base Camp: Camp Sea Gull. I grew comfortable and secure as personnel director. The rhythm and challenges of recruiting and training 250 summer camp staff became familiar and manageable. I developed close, long-lasting relationships with many of these bright, energetic young leaders. Successful seasons brought me increasing self-confidence as well as outside approval.

Life fell into a predictable routine. I quickened my pace, rushing along to accomplish more to ensure continuing success and promotions. The idea of eventually becoming director of the camp, planted in my thoughts at the time I was hired, began taking root. I envisioned expanding the program to a year-round operation that would include adults, seniors, families, and organizations.

Journal, January 1, 1980: **Marker Moment.** My mad dash toward this imagined future came to a halt when, following the retirement of the director, I was not selected as his successor. The new director was well qualified, having worked with the camp longer than anyone else. Although I had been led to presume things would be different, his appointment closed the door for me.

1. **Guide Note: Contemplation.** The announcement of a new director was an unanticipated shock. I began to let go of my dream of directing Sea Gull and turned to put on faith in the Spirit in the fragmented, bewildering world in which I found myself.

ADVENTURER

Journal, January 16, 1980: **Shifting Attention.**
Just as I was slowing down to adjust to this turn of
events, I received a letter inviting me to apply for
the director's position at Camp Sloane, a YMCA
camp in Lakeville, Connecticut. As I shifted my
attention, I saw that, by looking beyond my
immediate world of Camp Sea Gull, I might still be
able to realize my dream of becoming a camp
director.

Journal, February 13, 1980: **Detaching from
the Familiar.** My excitement quickly ebbed in the
screaming silence that followed the submission of
my résumé. After four weeks, the silence was
shattered with an official announcement of the
selection of someone else. I hadn't even merited
an interview. The long weeks of waiting eroded
the bulwark of my confidence. A deluge of doubt
undermined my vision of becoming a director of a
camp.

TRUST THE WILDNESS

Journal, February 26, 1980: **Freeing My Mind.**
At the American Camping Association National
Convention in Boston, I had coffee with the
camping consultant for the YMCA, who had
referred me to Camp Sloane. He listened
attentively to my disappointment in not being
seriously considered. His stories of Y
professionals who had become trapped and stale
in comfortable jobs soothed my wounds and
encouraged me to amend my assumptions about
my own path.

As we talked, I began to understand how my old
habits and expectations had closed my mind to
new possibilities. And I began to see the real
danger of getting stuck in the comfortable, well-
worn ruts on the path at Sea Gull. Then, with
words that I came to see as a sign, the consultant
nudged me to the very edge of my path. "You
have developed many gifts at Sea Gull that can

be useful in other Y camps," he said. "Such as Camp Becket," he added, by way of example.

Journal, February 27. 1980: **Resisting Change.**
His words had been a gratifying compliment, a much-needed boost for my ego. Becket was a well-respected boys' camp in the Berkshire Mountains of western Massachusetts that had served generations of campers. Flattered though I was, I was still closed to the possibility of change. Cille was enjoying a successful career in education. Our children were well adjusted and happy in their schools. I was on a secure, familiar path as personnel director. I dismissed this "sign" as just a wild idea.

Journal, February 28, 1980: **Leaving Home.**
The Y consultant introduced me to the CEO of the Two State YMCA, the administrator of Camp Becket. His description of Becket's rich history of spiritual formation and its progressive year-round

programming caught my attention. At the conclusion of our conversation, he informed me of a recent illness that necessitated his retiring as camp director. At last leaving my old home at Sea Gull, I was intrigued by his invitation to apply for the position.

Journal, March 2, 1980: **Opening My Heart.** Yet the possibility of really leaving my old path didn't really register until I shared this encounter with Cille on my return home. Her response surprised me. "Lloyd," she said, knowing my disappointment with the door that had recently closed on my dream, "there is something *more* in the timing of this invitation. I think you need to pay attention to it. Besides, I don't want to miss any opportunity to visit Boston."

Her enthusiasm cleansed my heart of its blinkered prejudices about the future and perpetual need to control every outcome. Inspired now to turn toward this new spirit I'd glimpsed stirring along the edges of my path, I sent in my letter of application. For the first time in years, I felt the sense of freedom that came with putting my faith in the spiritual energy moving in a new direction.

Journal, March 14, 1980: **Confronting Conflict.** Yet I had reached a critical fork in the path. I felt secure at Sea Gull, but staying on that path required giving up my intuition that something *more* was reaching out to me in this opportunity at Becket. The path toward Becket led in an appealing direction, but at the expense of the comfort and security that came with staying in my familiar place.

2. **Guide Note:** **Meditation.** In this conflict, I reoriented my mind toward matters of the Spirit—quiet matters, easily overlooked. My daily practice of journal keeping tuned down distracting claims on my attention,

allowing me to refocus on those elusive spiritual matters.

Journal, March 26, 1980: Refocusing on the Spirit. My next meeting with the Two State CEO renewed my hope in the Spirit. As I thumbed through brochures and newsletters filled with examples of spiritual growth taking place at camp, my heart stirred with excitement at his mention of my contributing, in my own way, "to the advancement of such a mission." His invitation for me to meet the board and key staff felt like an acknowledgement of what I was sensing in my heart.

Journal, April 9, 1980: Respecting My Heart. From that first meeting with the board of directors in Boston, I saw this path would be different. Founded in 1903, Camp Becket-in-the-Berkshires was one of the oldest continually running summer camps in the United States. Its lineage wove back to Henry Gibson, one of the pioneers in organized residential camping in this country.

Board members in business suits assembled around a gleaming mahogany table laden with porcelain coffee cups and pitchers of sparkling water. They made it clear that they had no intention of emulating Camp Sea Gull. They firmly believed Becket's small-group experience was the most effective way to shape character, and its model of cabins with eight campers and a counselor the ideal environment. Their deep commitment to spiritual formation became a refrain chiming in my own heart as I weighed my options.

Journal, April 18, 1980: Illumining the Path. I had until the end of the week to give Becket my answer. Returning from lunch on the final day, still stewing about which way to go, I met my minister leaving the Y. I spilled out my quandary. "Go in all haste," he told me, without a moment's hesitation. "It's a clear call."

But, I countered, what about housing—what about the dearth of jobs for teachers—what about the welfare of my children? His response was swift and sure. "You need to be grateful for the time you have had at Sea Gull. It has been wonderful preparation for this new opportunity. However, you are at the emotional end of your call here." Seeing my face fall and my eyes fill with fear, he added, "If you don't take this call, you will lose the vision that is coming to life in you right now. You can't return to your old job with any enthusiasm." Then with a hearty handshake and a pat on the back, he said, "Be grateful for this new opportunity God has brought to you," and went on his way.

This conversation amplified the light of my heart's intuitions, showing me the way. I *was* at the end of my path at Sea Gull; I saw that Becket was the right direction for me. I mailed a letter that afternoon accepting the offer.

Journal, May 29, 1980: Coming to a Crossroad. Barely a month later, the director of Camp Sea Gull surprised everyone by announcing his plan to retire immediately. He appealed to my sense of loyalty to stay with the camp to ease the transition to new leadership.

I was caught between my head's notions of duty to Sea Gull and my heart's attraction to Becket. Some days I felt boldly confident about striking off in a new direction, sure that I was responding to the authentic movement of the Spirit. Other days I fretted about disappointing my colleagues and abandoning security and friendship for some risky pie-in-the-sky dream. My tyrannical "inner pharaohs" fought every step of the way to hold me captive to my fear of failure and rejection.

TRUST THE WILDNESS

<u>Journal, July 23, 1980:</u> Persevering in the Spirit. The decisive showdown came during a visit from a Catholic priest with whom I had developed a friendship over the winter. He had companioned me during the discernment of going to Becket with an ear open to my doubts and an eye focused on the Spirit's movement. He had guided me to hold on to my intuition when I was tempted to turn back.

When he visited camp, I told him of my wavering about Becket. He invited Cille and me to a quiet space just away from the bustling activity of camp. Putting his hands gently on our heads, he blessed our mission to Camp Becket. His words, etched in my memory, confirmed my understanding of the Spirit's movement. "Your real work is now in Boston," he said. "Go—your move is right." With his commissioning, a veil dropped from my eyes, revealing the holy intentions embedded in my struggle.

ADVENTURER

Journal, August 8, 1980: **Finding a New Way.**
Cille, our son, Christopher, and I had gone to
Massachusetts to make final preparations for the
move. The inner pharaohs staged one more
skirmish to try to hold me hostage to my doubts
and fears. We had no house in Boston; our house
in Raleigh had no buyer; and Cille had no job.
When Christopher and I attended a weekend at
Camp Becket, I became overwhelmed with the
breadth of responsibilities and challenges that
were now mine as I stepped into the shoes of the
highly respected former director. No matter how
stultifying I'd found my old path at Sea Gull, it was
at least secure and predictable.

Then, as I sat in a real estate office making a
down payment on a house in Medfield,
Massachusetts, hesitantly making my way
through the paper work, knowing it would be
impossible to carry two mortgages, a telephone

TRUST THE WILDNESS

call brought news that our home in Raleigh had sold. That serendipitous timing reaffirmed my sense that something right and true was leading me toward Camp Becket.

Now, with all our possessions piled in a moving van, the entire family—Christopher, Cille and me, our daughter, Meredith, and Cinnamon, the beagle—squeezed into our Volkswagen Rabbit and headed north. Cille still had no job; I had one, but feared it was over my head; our children were beginning new schools with no one they knew; and we were all leaving our support system of friends and family hundreds of miles behind. Homesickness infected us all.

But I was not alone! In spite of all the outer obstacles and inner trials, I was at peace with this move. The visit to Boston had been revelatory, alluding to a transcendent meaning beyond itself. My consciousness had been altered by the vision of directing Camp Becket. A new and right spirit had been born in me. I felt reconnected with something greater than myself, aligned with the movement of the Spirit in my life.

Journal, April 17, 1981: **Getting Stuck.** I started at Becket full of enthusiasm, eager to try my wings. But soon I was mired in a power struggle that had me doubting whether I really had heard the Spirit's longings after all. In the six months following my acceptance of the camp director's position, the former director's health had improved. He was reluctant to relinquish the reins of authority. His wife, the director of the girls' camp, brought his voice to our discussions, sharing their vision and dreams for the camps. I was ready to move in; he was not ready to move on; and she had to work with both of us. I was tempted to turn back to my old path at Sea Gull.

3. **Guide Note:** **Discernment.** I put on love for the Spirit, following its movement into the real world. Bringing all I had learned about the Spirit's presence and all I understood about my authentic self into my choices, I discovered the Spirit leading me further along in the direction I'd taken. I recognized the Spirit's longings, not just my own, drawing me into a new story.

Journal, August 12, 1981: **Revering the Spirit.** My renewed trust in things of the Spirit came in response to a camper's accusation of inappropriate touching by a trip leader—a seasoned counselor—on an overnight hike. After reviewing the accusation, I suspected that something inappropriate had indeed gone on, but the counselor unequivocally denied any wrongdoing. With no witnesses, accurate information was elusive.

ADVENTURER

Two senior administrators differed on the right response. One, a school psychologist, strongly defended the counselor, insisting he should remain at camp. The other, a pediatrician, advised removing the counselor until more substantial information could be obtained. I was stalemated.

This was new territory for me. Up to this point my professional life had been spent on close-knit teams where unanimity in decisions was expected. With such clear disagreement among responsible adults, compromise seemed impossible. My illusions of finding consensus crumbled in frustration at the stubbornness of the two administrators. I walked out of the office realizing *I* would have to change.

I shifted my attention from worrying about approval to relying on my own perceptions. Returning to the campsite where the incident was alleged to have occurred, I listened to everyone involved: the camper, the trip leader, the cabin counselor, the trip leader's supervisor, and the two administrators. Acknowledging these disparate points of view clarified the complexity of the situation. I recognized the blindness my own need for approval had created. Freed from that constraint, I saw the decision as a matter of judgment rather than consensus. I opened to the stirrings in my heart and removed the trip leader to protect the camper.

Journal, September 3, 1981: Responding to the Spirit. Yet I continued to feel as though my intuitions were being strangled. I spilled out my frustrations to one of my mentors, who was leading a workshop at Family Camp. Having companioned me at other moments on my spiritual journey, she recognized in those frustrations my thirst for approval and my familiar pattern of trying to get it by pleasing others.

ADVENTURER

Listening more than talking, she finally confronted me with the reality of this terrain. "Lloyd," she said, "you are never going to be able to make things right in this situation!"

With the skill of an expert guide, she led me beyond my old self back to my heart. Growing up, I had been taught to follow my head. For me, that had come to mean getting what I wanted by making things right for others. This attitude was leading me away from my own thoughts and feelings, blinding me to the Spirit's movement.

She pointed me in a different direction, inviting me to trust the stirrings in my heart. Responding to these intuitions drew me to a deeper awareness—a spiritual longing that was not my own. My awareness of this inner, spiritual dimension was renewed.

TRUST THE WILDNESS

<u>Journal, September 22, 1981:</u> Walking in the Soul's Light. I also shared my feelings of frustration in letting go of ingrained patterns with the Green Water Sailing Society, a group I'd spent time with since 1978 when we came together for a three-day sailing cruise in Pamlico Sound in eastern North Carolina. The experience was so exhilarating and the fellowship so inspiring that five of us had made it an annual event. The intense wilderness challenges and the close quarters of the cruising vessel turned casual friends into close spiritual companions.

Responding to my despair, they reminded me that I needed to *trust the compass*. This was good advice for sailors who cruise for hours on wide, coastal waters, out of sight of familiar landmarks. The position of the sun, an unidentified buoy in the distance, or the glimpse of a far shore could easily become a temptation to change course. Learning to trust the compass, the vessel's navigational guide (this was before the days of GPS), despite distractions led to safe harbor time and time again.

I had to learn to trust the Spirit resonating in my heart as my navigational guide, to let it be my compass. As I refocused on its readings, I saw holy intentions, not just my own, leading me to Becket. I had a deeper awareness of the Spirit's call to this mission. It was the right place for me at this time.

Journal, February 7, 1984: **Enduring a Dark Night.** The power struggle came to a head when another heart attack put the CEO in the hospital for two weeks and out of the office for four more. His administrative duties and budget responsibilities involved day-to-day operations, which could be left unattended for only so long. His wife temporarily assumed those administrative duties.

TRUST THE WILDNESS

My exclusion from budget decisions became an increasing handicap for me during his absence, but to object would be to enter dangerous territory. One business manager had already lost his job for questioning the budget process. With a young family dependent on me for financial support, I was reluctant to move into that dark, unknown area.

Journal, April 12, 1984: Obeying My Heart. One day, riding to a committee meeting with a camp parent who served on both the camp and the association boards, I caught a glimmer of new light. As I told him of my growing frustrations in being excluded from the budget process, his comprehensive knowledge of camp finances became obvious. "Budgets," he responded, "are about empowerment, not position."

He was right. I was inspired by his observation to make changes to the budget in spite of the dangers I perceived. I came to see that the budget, which I had considered a nuisance binding my hands, was actually a way of moving out of my organizational predicament. Trusting my intuition, I prepared a new budget, separating out areas that specifically affected leadership, programs, and facilities at the camp, and sent a proposal to the board.

Journal, April 17, 1984: Trusting the Wildness. The board responded affirmatively, adopting my recommendations. The reorganization of budget accountability joined my vision of directing camp with the resources to implement it, empowering my call.

Journal, August 14, 1984: Becoming an Adventurer. My colleagues and I continued to differ on priorities over time off, salaries, and discipline. I was often temped to look first for what they wanted and then to try to appease them. But,

TRUST THE WILDNESS

acting on faith—trusting my compass—I had grown spiritually. Our relationship had changed from a power struggle to a creative alliance. We now faced our challenges together.

The camp flourished. New cabins were built, old boats replaced, and a new creative arts building erected. More schools, families, and organizations were attracted to our programs, increasing our service to the community.

I had become an adventurer on the spiritual journey, conforming to the movement of the Spirit in my actions. I had found my heart-path. I had grown to possess my own life—my true way in the world at this time. In spite of ongoing problems and challenges, I had an abiding sense of being at the right place, at the right time, doing the right thing.

ADVENTURER

Ponder
1. See everything as a portent. Examine everyday encounters in search of signs.
2. Identify your obstacles. Refocus your attention to see your way around the barriers in your path.
3. Test the spirits; look at them in the context of your understanding of scripture and the Christian tradition. Share your promptings with a spiritual friend.
4. Go slow. Give the process of discernment as much time as it needs until a choice emerges with clarity. Look for the next step forward, not the final destination.
5. Imagine the fruits of engaging your vision. A well-discerned decision will result in good fruits that improve life and make it better. It will bring freedom, healing, direction, and purpose to your life.

PILGRIM

Keep awake and pray that you may not come into a time of trial; the spirit indeed is willing, but the flesh is weak. Mark 14:38

Base Camp: Camp Becket-in-the-Berkshires.
Responsibility for the budget had empowered my call to Camp Becket. I was enthusiastic about the positive impact that a good staff of about 100 dedicated young leaders was having with this community of 260 campers. The camp, divided by age level into four villages, was built with an intentional focus on simplicity. The cabins were rustic, with no electricity. Flashlights and candles reinforced the experience of retreating from the world of commercial dependency.

PILGRIM

Daily mindfulness of the Spirit's presence gradually replaced my old faith in "right" beliefs. Prayer and journal keeping formed a "rule of life" that kept me awake to a spiritual presence. I became more steadfast in my faith, continuing to strip off layers my old self with its antiquated practices and clothing myself with knowledge of the Spirit.

Journal, August 3, 1986: **Marker Moment.** A candle in Cabin Glacier burned down, igniting the wall behind it. By the time I heard the alarm and ran to the scene, the entire building was engulfed in flames. I watched in helpless horror as the cabin burned to the ground, trembling at the thought that someone might be trapped inside. The nightmare of losing a camper or counselor haunted me long after a frantic search confirmed that all were safe.

TRUST THE WILDNESS

1. **Guide Note: Prayer.** In prayer, I put on faith *and* hope in the Spirit, shifting my attention away from the many diversions that tended to drown out It's voice. Going to bed earlier in order to get up sooner, I found a place of solitude with fewer distractions. I entered this time of prayer with a genuine desire to release my own story and my attachments to preconceived outcomes and to attune myself to the Spirit.

Journal, August 3, 1986: Shifting Attention.
Old wooden structures with candles for lighting were accidents waiting to happen. In spite of my most conscientious efforts, a devastating fire occurred. It had destroyed not just the building, but my confidence in my ability to control the outcome. Guilt at disappointing others pushed aside any lingering illusions I had of being in charge.

PILGRIM

Journal, August 5, 1986: **Detaching from the Familiar.** I shared my paralyzing guilt with a Unitarian minister, a member of the camp board. As we talked, he walked me to edge of the parched path where familiar concerns for failure blocked my openness to the Spirit. With a probing question he broke through the bondage of guilt my conditioning had imposed on me, and invited me to consider providential possibilities that exceeded my perception of personal failure. Loosened from my fear of disappointing others, I became more attentive to the holy presence even in the context of a tragedy.

Journal, August 18, 1986: **Freeing My Mind.** As my guilt dissipated and I was able to become more conscious of life around me, a graduate program in counseling psychology at Lesley University caught my attention. There seemed to be a serendipitous connection between Lesley's focus on integrating mind, body, and spirit and the

YMCA's mission. I found myself being pulled beyond my familiar path in organized camping toward this sign of something *more.*

Journal, August 27, 1986: **Resisting Change.** Yet leaving my familiar path to pursue this sign proved difficult. When I requested continuing education funds to enroll in graduate school, I received a tepid, cautious consent. The CEO suggested that a business degree would be more useful. That mere whiff of disapproval sent my inner pharaohs on a rampage. Fear of disappointing him tempted me to pull back and continue on the safe—but burned out—path at Becket.

Journal, September 10, 1986: **Leaving Home.** I shared my reservations about trying graduate school with the Green Water Sailing Society during our fall sail. Their enthusiasm for this turn in my path pushed aside my reluctance to disappoint my employer. I left my familiar home of camping to pay attention to the new stirring in my heart.

Journal, September 22, 1986: Opening My Heart. Cleansed of my anxious efforts to control my destiny, I was inspired to enter Lesley, personally financing my tuition. Turning aside from my familiar path at camp, I arrived at the first of two evening classes, feeling like a college student again, wiggling out of an existence that no longer fit.

Journal, August, 27, 1987: Confronting Conflict. Obstacles appeared when I asked for continuing-education funds for a second year at Lesley. My request included an additional academic course plus a required half-day clinical practicum. This extra academic commitment forced my request to be referred to the chairman of the board. What had been a simple matter suddenly assumed broader career implications, threatening my employment. I was tempted to abandon my hope of completing my degree and just stick with the camp path.

2. **Guide Note:** **Journal Keeping.** In the solitude of morning prayers, I set my mind on what I was drawn to in scriptural meditations and was intentional in recording the insights, questions, and feelings that arose. In the evening, journaling the significant events of the day became an opportunity for noticing where I had responded or failed to respond to the Spirit's presence glimpsed during times of prayer. Reflecting on these entries, I came to recognize a larger pattern. Events and encounters were transfigured by the infusion of the soul's light, revealing the movement of the Spirit.

I did not see different things; rather, I saw things differently. Responding to the Spirit meant I was no longer following a path that was laid out and structured, but was charting a new path altogether—my true way. I was pulling together new possibilities in ways that others might not understand or feel able to support.

Journal, August 28, 1987: **Refocusing on the Spirit.** My courses in counseling psychology had renewed my respect for the truth of the inner life. Robert Kegan's *The Evolving Self,* Daniel Levinson's *The Seasons of a Man's Life,* and Carl Roger's *Becoming a Person* expanded my appreciation for the "heart" beyond its use as a contemporary synonym for feelings. It came to represent a deeper level of consciousness where memory, experience, thoughts, hopes, feelings, desires, intentions, and intuitions join to form character. Journaling refocused my attention on this deeper consciousness beyond the expectations and assumptions of reason's sight.

Journal, August 29, 1987: Respecting My Heart. I caught a glimpse of this deeper awareness in a conversation with one of my mentors. At Family Camp where she was leading a seminar, I brought her up to date on my renewed respect for the inner life I was discovering in my courses at Lesley. As we talked about where this was leading, she reaffirmed her interest in having me join her counseling practice when I completed my degree. This opportunity rekindled my dream of counseling, drawing me further along the path at Lesley.

Journal, September 3, 1987: Illumining the Path. The Chelsea Counseling Center, a well-established community practice in suburban Boston, accepted me for clinical training. Still reluctant about meeting with the chairman, I explained to a friend on the Y board the obstacles I was encountering in arranging time to fulfill the practicum. His enthusiasm for the exceptional opportunity for clinical training offered at Chelsea surprised me. His confidence swayed me.

I met with the chairman of the board, who approved my request for funds to continue the program. This support reassured me that this path at Lesley, even though I didn't know where it would lead, was the right direction.

Journal, January 22, 1988: Coming to a Crossroad. The size of hurdles increased when I had to fulfill the requirement for a two-semester, eight-hour-per-week internship. This additional workload tilted the delicate balance I had established between the two paths I was traveling. Attempting to maintain that balance, I submitted a proposal to work in the camp office on Saturdays in order to serve at the counseling center during the week. The swiftness of its rejection enticed me to turn back from the soul's light illuminating this path.

Journal, March 20, 1988: Persevering in the Spirit. I found my way through this crossroad with fidelity to the intuitions in my heart. I offered to reduce my time out of the camp office by extending the length of my internship, a proposal the camp's administrative committee immediately shot down. Shaken by this second rejection, I blurted out my doubts about the authenticity of my intuitions to a psychologist friend at coffee following Sunday worship. She reminded me that risky situations were integral parts of spiritual growth, and that responding to them opened the way forward. Her reassurance fortified my steadfastness in seeking a solution for the internship.

Journal, May 24, 1988: **Finding a New Way.** A third proposal came from the CEO, who suggested I change to part-time status for nine months and hire an assistant to cover my camp responsibilities. My reduced salary would pay for the increase in staff. This drastic step of reducing my salary and responsibility with no assurance of a better position with a master's in psychology tempted me to give up on the academic path.

As I anguished over this decision, a letter arrived from my supervisor at the counseling center confirming my progress during the practicum. His words illumined more than my performance. They revived my intuition that finishing the degree was the right track for me.

The CEO stopped by my office to ascertain my reaction should the administrative committee turn down this new proposal. Though my head warned me to be cautious, to respond in a way that would please him and protect my future with the camp, the pull of my heart was stronger. Clinging to that deep sense of rightness, I declared my intention to accept the internship and complete the degree.

The proposal was approved. In a flash, the disparate strands of my heart's longings coalesced. Intangible, spiritual desires became part of my tangible, material world. My consciousness was altered by the intuitions in my heart. A new spirit of counsel that had been evolving in my imagination was now fully formed, augmenting my earlier vision of control. I had been anointed with a vision—a manifestation of the Spirit in my life. I felt aligned with the movement of the Spirit and at peace with this new path.

Journal, December 22, 1989: Traversing a Parched Land. This transition from my head to my heart led me away from Camp Becket and

PILGRIM

back to North Carolina, where I joined my former mentor in a marriage and family counseling practice in New Bern. The independence of private practice had been wildly appealing after years in the cumbersome hierarchy of the YMCA. Very soon, however, loneliness cast a long shadow over my enthusiasm. I missed association with colleagues and, even more, the organizational structure and routines that clearly defined daily expectations. A relentless quiet, like a tomb, settled on my office.

A full complement of work would have dispelled my despondency. Unfortunately, it never materialized. Referrals were few and insurance requirements limited the availability of new clients. Empty appointment slots fueled my anxiety. As my savings account dwindled, doubts intruded on the faith I had followed here. In the deepening financial darkness, I had to choose whether to hold on to the Spirit's vision or return to more conventional wisdom.

3. **Guide Note:** **Discernment.** I put on love for the Spirit, listening for its movement and clothing myself in its knowledge. Responding to my soul's light, I was drawn to recognize holy longings to move in a new direction.

Journal, January 12, 1990: **Revering the Spirit.** The CEO of the Raleigh Y invited me to return to Sea Gull as camp director. Although this unexpected opportunity promised financial security—a godsend!—I was frightened. At Camp Becket, I had grown to appreciate the uniqueness of the spiritual life. At Lesley, I had developed skills for listening to my heart. This new direction would lead straight back into the tightly managed organization that had previously threatened my spiritual growth.

I surrendered my hesitancy following a call from the director of camping services. The Y board had separated the director's position from its initial inclusion as part of the CEO's responsibilities. This change had created a critical need for an experienced director—me—and staff to live and work year-round at the camp, expanding programs and services. Not only that, I could begin immediately serving as a consultant in developing new programs for the outdoor center. These signs reinforced my feeling of the Sprit's presence in this opportunity.

Journal, March 15, 1990: Responding to the Spirit. My horizons expanded as I followed my heart's intuitions. As part of my counseling practice, I contracted with a middle school to facilitate a leadership-development program for underprivileged students. After exploring many program options, I implemented a curriculum similar to the adventure-based activities that had worked so well at Camp Becket. In the midst of a student's animated reaction to a trust-fall exercise, I perceived my personal preference for outdoor-adventure activities, rather than individual therapy, as a tool for personal growth.

I discovered a genuine joy working with enthusiastic students and committed teachers in this kind of experiential-education situation. Such activities tended to open me up and make me more available to myself, to others, and to the Spirit. I felt most truly myself. Rather than draining me, these activities released a fresh energy, even when the job was difficult and demanding.

Journal, August 25, 1990: Walking in the Soul's Light. Still, my concern with losing my integrity in the morass of a large organization continued to choke my enthusiasm for returning to a YMCA camp. A close friend with whom I had been sailing for many years reminded me of what

PILGRIM

I had learned earlier at Becket: In any large organization, budget accountability was the real source of authority and responsibility. Light broke through the clouds of uncertainty, revealing a way back to the camping path that could preserve my integrity.

I met with the CEO to discuss the specifics of the new position of camp director. I reached a dangerous precipice when he refused to consider any changes to the organizational structure that would clarify my role. Strong as my desire to return to camp was, I was not about to abandon my vision to the rigid restrictions of the organization. In lieu of a change in structure, I proposed a change in budget accountability.

His response surprised me. Although unwilling to change the lines of reporting, he was open to modifying my job description to include greater budget accountability. With this modification, I felt drawn to recognize God's longings, not just my own, in returning to the camp path. I had a deeper awareness that camp was right direction for me. It was my mission. I accepted the invitation to return to Camp Sea Gull.

Journal, September 29, 1990: Enduring a Dark Night. I was enthusiastic about expanding programs in the spring and fall seasons. The assistant directors, however, were not happy at the idea of pulling up stakes and living at camp year round to do so. Their resistance created a cloud of uncertainty around my mission, tempting me to stop rather than upset them.

Journal, December 8, 1991: Obeying My Heart. The staff's growing discontent over relocating led to serious reservations about the camp's long-range plan to expand services. These doubts found a collective voice at a meeting of the camp committee. During a lengthy discussion about whether to change the proposed plan of program growth, a new alternative eventually emerged: Current staff would be encouraged, but not required, to move; new staff would be employed with the understanding that they would work from camp year round.

Acting on faith, I leaped for the modification. With this change the plan to expand programs and relocate the office was reconfirmed. While this was not the way I had envisioned the outcome, the compromise released energy in me that had been stymied by the conflict.

Journal, December 9, 1991: Trusting the Wildness. I rediscovered my heart-path. A holy vision of camp directing had been reconnected with a sacred call at a particular time and place. This infusion of the Holy Spirit healed the fragmentation that threatened my progress when I had been enticed to turn back. Growing in knowledge of a holy will, I was empowered to move forward as camp director.

Journal, March 7, 1992: Becoming a Pilgrim.
The renewal of my heart-path was not the end of struggles and uncertainty. Calamitous events continued to challenge and change the direction of the heart-path. Obstacles—both social and psychological—blocked the path, tempting me to abandon course.

But I had grown in soulfulness. I was a pilgrim living in a spiritual kingdom, maintaining a spiritual perspective by a rule of life, prayerfully journaling daily activities. I continued steadfast in faith in the Spirit, rooted and grounded in the soul's light. Reflecting more than reacting, I paid attention to signs, intuitions, and promptings. I understood the movement of the Spirit in inspirations and visions in my life, and I was guided by its calls. I continued on my true way.

PILGRIM

Ponder

1. What habitual ways of seeing challenge your devotion to the Spirit? What personal fears hook your attention, pulling you away from things of the Spirit?
2. What disciplines—practices—help you stay vigilant in refocusing on the soul's light?
3. To what signs, intuitions, or promptings are you responding at this time?
4. What are the fruits of mindful living, of being more contemplative in your actions?
5. How has your understanding of the Holy changed during your journey?

GUIDE

The wind blows where it chooses, but you do not know where it comes from or where it goes. So it is with everyone who is born of the Spirit.
John 3:8

Base Camp: Camp Sea Gull. I came to understand that the Holy is everywhere—ever-present— and I was beginning to live in that awareness. However, I found myself in an end-time where others who could say those words of a living God were cut off from their meaning by a cultural shift that blurred the sacred presence. In this time when political, economic, social, and religious systems seemed to be shifting, I was drawn to proclaim the nearness of this spiritual kingdom and guide others to find their way to it.

GUIDE

Following the decision to continue the camp's long-range plan of program expansion, the offices and some professional staff moved on site. New programs in the spring and fall extended services to the surrounding communities.

The two previous directors had been heavily involved with managing all aspects of the summer camp—place, program, and leadership. As the new director, I was bursting with enthusiasm, eager to follow in their successful footsteps. But as programs grew and more staff were employed, the terrain was changing. I raced along the path those directors had carved out like a horse with blinders, far too centered on my own success to notice a change in the movement of the Spirit.

Journal, February 7, 1996: Marker Moment. On my way to another hectic day, I fainted at the wheel of our station wagon, crossed a lane of oncoming traffic, and smacked head-on into a large tree. When I regained consciousness three days later, I squinted through the window of a room in the intensive care unit of Craven Regional Medical Center and then assessed the damage: multiple broken bones, my jaw sealed shut by wires, and my life maintained by a ventilator. Close to death for twenty-one days, I was taking an imposed a leave of absence, relinquishing— willingly or not—earlier assumptions and expectations about my future.

1. **Guide Note: Contemplation.** Morning prayer and journal keeping established a rhythm, a rule of life, that supported my orientation inward, putting on faith in the Spirit's presence in the midst of this accident.

Journal, July 3, 1996: Shifting Attention. When I was finally able to return to camp duties, I continued letting go of the wisdom I had acquired from my predecessors. I received an advisory from the Pamlico Emergency Management Response Team to evacuate camp in the face of an approaching hurricane. The camp had a long history of riding out big storms, but Bertha was different. Her intensity and projected path required a change in standard operating procedures. It had been forty years since a storm had forced such a departure, but the day before the storm's projected arrival, I made the call to move all campers and staff inland to safety.

Journal, July 25, 1996: **Detaching from the Familiar.** Hard on the heels of the hurricane, an extensive fish kill in the Neuse River attracted national attention, uncovering environmental problems with water quality. The culprit, the microscopic organism *Pfisteria,* was not only a threat to aquatic life, but, according to one scientist, to human health as well. Campers sent alarming letters to their parents describing the hundreds of fish carcasses littering the shore. Recognizing that my habitual need for approval had to give way to the greater need for protecting campers and staff, I initiated a daily water-quality monitoring program.

Journal, April 20, 2000: **Freeing My Mind.** In spite of these steps forward, releasing my habits and assumptions about my role continued to be a slow process. My escape came, ironically, in a prison cell. I had travelled to South Africa to plan an experience in international travel for the older campers. Following an immersion in the natural wildness of Kruger National Park and the political wildness of Cape Town, as people searched for new ways to bring political order out of cultural chaos, I experienced a profound spiritual wildness on Robben Island, where Nelson Mandela had been imprisoned for resisting British rule. Standing in the small, bare cell where he had spent so many years in exile, I perceived with sudden clarity my own imprisonment within the outdated assumptions and beliefs I had acquired from the former directors. I stepped out of Mandela's cell armed with determination to break free of my own self-imposed incarceration.

Journal, August 18, 2000: Resisting Change.
The camp's CEO invited me to become the director of camping services, a more administrative role. This proposal wreaked havoc with my acquired assumptions about being a hands-on manager. My narrow-minded inner pharaohs returned with all their prejudices, slamming my mind shut. I declined the invitation.

Journal, September 19, 2001: Leaving Home.
When one of my former assistants was appointed director of camping services, making him my supervisor, I was jarred loose from the "privileged" perspective I'd assumed. This role reversal flushed out my previous assumptions and pushed

them to a new level of consciousness. At last, I opened my mind to listen with compassion rather than compulsion—and heard, for the first time, concern for the future of the camp over the din of my own fear of change. Fresh energy enabled me to give up my anxious attempts to hold on to the imagined security of the past.

Journal, October 9, 2002: **Opening My Heart.** A year later, the director of camping services resigned. I had by then abandoned my old expectations and refocused my attention on the future of the camp. In discussions with the CEO, we decided that the best way to tackle our long-term goals for the camp would be to split the director of camping services job into two new positions, executive director and assistant director. I would become the executive director, combining the task of overall camp direction with new duties in a capital campaign; the assistant director would take on hands-on program management, freeing me for my additional administrative responsibilities.

My heart, cleansed of its conventional wisdom, was open to perceive this as a sign to move on. I had been delivered from bondage in the parched land of acquired beliefs. Turning aside to attend to the Spirit, I perceived the wildness, the infusion of something *more* into my vision as camp director.

Journal, March 9, 2003: **Confronting Conflict.** As part of my preparation for retirement, I took a week off to attend a course in spiritual direction in the lifelong learning program at Columbia Theological Seminary in Decatur, Georgia. There I quickly learned the difference between the values education in which I had long been engaged and intimacy with the Spirit.

The concept of an intimate relationship with the Spirit conflicted with the orthodox beliefs I had learned at divinity school and the values implied in those doctrines I was teaching at camp. My training in right beliefs left little room for such intimacy. My roommate during this course, a pastor from Wilmington, was so challenged by the experiential language that he left after two days. While I was tempted to go with him, my airline ticket had been reserved for the end of the course.

2. **Guide Note: Meditation.** At Columbia Theological Seminary I was introduced to practices that led to the Spirit and kept me open and responsive to its mysterious movement in my heart and in the world. In the midst of this conflict between orthodoxy and intimacy, I put on hope in the Spirit, refocusing on the insights it inspired.

Journal, September 25, 2003: Refocusing on the Spirit. I hit the ceiling of my camping career when, during the process of budget development,

I reached the top of my salary range. In lieu of salary increases, I was given a stipend to prepare for retirement.

This bend in the path turned my attention back to Columbia and the thesis I was completing for the course in spiritual direction. The holy intimacy I had been introduced to in this course quenched a spiritual thirst that doctrines and values education had not. Wanting *more*, I was attracted by the exploration of the Christian tradition of spirituality offered in the graduate certificate program. The stipend could help finance my studies.

Journal, January 29, 2004: Respecting My Heart. A weeklong Immersion Experience began my introduction to spiritual practices in this tradition. Classroom lectures examined faith practices in the Old and New Testaments and in the monastic and reformed traditions that focused attention on the Spirit. Prayer, scriptural meditation, and discernment were vehicles that led to an increased understanding of a spiritual dimension of life and heightened intimacy with the Holy Spirit.

One afternoon as I walked the labyrinth in the quiet of Harrington Center Chapel, I was seized with an unmistakable sense of something *more*. Later that evening, as I prepared an outline of my spiritual autobiography, I grasped the kinship of that perception of a mysterious presence with similar experiences I'd had at Camp Sequoia, Camp Sea Gull, and Camp Becket; each formed a bead on a sacred string. In all of these heart-felt moments, I had awakened to a deeper truth.

Journal, April 21, 2004: Illumining the Path. My second elective in the certificate program was a course in contemplative spirituality. I joined the Trappist community at the Monastery of the Holy Spirit in Conyers, Georgia. For a week, in the

deep silence of the monastery, I practiced
Centering Prayer, releasing attachments to
conventional wisdom to focus on the presence of
the Holy.

Late one afternoon as I journaled in the
monastery garden, the knolling of the chapel
chimes for vespers caught my attention. As I
turned to listen, a gentle breeze brushed aside
notes I had made from the afternoon lecture,
uncovering an article by Thomas Merton. Merton
advocated a return to the contemplative
experience as a way for contemporary,
technologically oriented believers to reconnect
with their spiritual depth. This serendipitous
whisper of the wind plus the warmth of the rock
wall on which I was leaning helped me see *more,*
inspiring me to cultivate a greater awareness of
the divine dimension.

TRUST THE WILDNESS

Journal, April 25, 2005: **Trusting in Intuition.**
These moments of inspiration were further
clarified a year later in a course called Mysticism
and Resistance. The course began with a review
of the historical resistance to experiential realities
beyond physical or intellectual apprehension. It
moved on to trace their presence in accounts of
mystical encounters in scripture as well as the
classical paths of spirituality that evolved from
scripture. These mystical moments revealed
something ultimately truer and more authentic
than acquired beliefs. They were preeminent
moments in the spiritual journey, illumining the
movement of the Spirit in life.

Journal, July 17, 2005: **Seeking the Spirit.** On
May 31, I retired from Camp Sea Gull, grateful for
the camp experience and energized by my
increasing appreciation for the significance of
intuitive feelings. I realized that the doctrines I had
acquired and values I had been teaching often

discounted recognition of and respect for the stirrings of my heart. While those cherished beliefs witnessed to a deeper spiritual dimension of life, they did not contain it.

Another class at Columbia on the desert fathers and mothers of the early Christian church guided me toward practices for accessing the deeper dimension. These mystics fled to the barren solitude of the desert to escape the distractions of civilization and the bondage of imperial rule in order to be more attentive to the work of the Spirit in their lives. Their stories of encounters with the Divine in that solitude inspired me to cultivate habits that would further open me to this holy dimension.

Journal, September 23, 2005: Journal Keeping. My next course, Spirituality for the Second Half of Life, introduced me to spiritual rules in the Benedictine, Ignatian, and Franciscan monastic orders as well as several contemporary patterns of practice. As I reflected on the many different ways of attending to the movement of the Spirit, I realized that journal keeping had served as my guide to mystical moments. The journaling format slowed me down, allowing me to become more contemplative in my actions. The process of reflecting on significant daily encounters transfigured those events with an infusion of soul's light that revealed the movement of the Spirit.

Journal, March 22, 2006: Coming to a Crossroad. To fulfill a practicum in the certificate program, I facilitated two groups for Centering Prayer at First Presbyterian Church in New Bern, North Carolina, where I was serving as parish associate. Each week the groups discussed various aspects and challenges of this discipline and devoted time to practicing it.

GUIDE

Maintaining periods of silence, reading scripture meditatively, and sharing personal experiences with a companion proved to be awkward for the participants. Their allegiance to inherited beliefs made them suspicious of turning inward to value their own perceptions over the authority of prevailing tradition. They, like many of their postmodern, scientifically informed contemporaries, were hesitant about intuitive knowing.

Their resistance to such "heart knowledge" in turn became an obstacle to my continuing with the contemplative practices I was learning at Columbia. A familiar personal pharaoh, vainglory, threatened my progress. Fearing disapproval, I was tempted to discount the authenticity of my own intuitions and turn back from the contemplative path.

TRUST THE WILDNESS

Journal, September 24, 2006: **Persevering in the Spirit.** But I held on to the intuitions resonating in my heart, and made a pilgrimage to Iona, the final requirement in the certificate program. I joined a group from Columbia making our visit to this small, windswept island off the west coast of Scotland, a "thin place," where for centuries pilgrims have found that the "membrane between the spiritual and material worlds is transparent."

Journal, September 28, 2006: **Finding a New Way.** The absence of schedules and vehicles and the pervasive stillness on the island were unsettling at first. But soon I fell into a natural rhythm of morning and evening worship in the Abbey, prayerful contemplation in the natural quiet, and journaling daily activities that restored my sensitivity to the Spirit's presence in all things.

GUIDE

The theme for the Thursday evening liturgy in the Abbey was commitment to God's will. An invitation to surrender resonated with me in the opening hymn:

> *Will you come and follow me, if I but call your name?*
> *Will you go where you don't know, and never be the same?*
> *Will you let my love be shown, will you let my name be known,*
> *Will you let my life be grown in you and you in me?*

Those lilting words summoned me to a place I didn't know—the place of mystical experience, beyond my head's knowledge, in the spiritual dimension where God's love is shown, where God's name is known, where God's life is grown in me.

TRUST THE WILDNESS

This place of mystical experience was the kingdom of God. It was near at hand, and the contemplative practices I had learned at Columbia had led me to it. A new spirit was born in me at that moment. A teacher of conventional beliefs and values had been transformed into a mystic, practicing ways of contemplation. These practices opened my heart to hear and understand the Spirit, restoring me to its movement in my life. A peace enveloped me at the conclusion of the hymn; I was aligned with a deeper truth in my life.

Journal, November 18, 2007: Living in an End-Time. But I soon found myself walking straight into the thorns of the culture that blinded modern people to the integrity of their own spiritual depths. I awoke in this briar patch when, with my new vision of the mystical kingdom of God still fresh, I began planning a return to Iona as part of my duties as parish associate at First Presbyterian Church.

GUIDE

Initially the idea of a trip to Scotland, the birthplace of Presbyterianism, ignited much interest in the congregation. But as the trip became better defined as a pilgrimage focused on experiencing the Holy rather than a sightseeing tour, enthusiasm waned. I was worried about finding enough participants to make the pilgrimage practical.

Something in the culture had shifted over time, creating the same conflict between head and heart that I had struggled with at Columbia. Like me, many of those to whom I appealed had grown up with a traditional view of earth as the center of creation and a supernatural, judgmental, interventionist God who manipulated—or chose not to manipulate—everything from a remote vantage point in heaven. Jesus was God's definitive action, opening the way to the place where the Holy was believed to dwell.

TRUST THE WILDNESS

But, like me, my potential pilgrims had been spellbound and forever changed by the advent of space travel and the extraordinary original views of earth from the moon. The Hubble telescope showed us an expanding and seemingly endless universe that relegated Planet Earth to a minute place in it. This new perspective challenged the conventional view of a three-tiered, heaven-earth-hell, cosmos that placed the Holy high and away in some remote region separate from creation.

Frightened and confused by this new information, some abandoned hope for the Holy altogether while others tightened their grip on traditional language, closing their minds to the thin places where the Spirit drew closer. Bondage to orthodox beliefs alienated them from the deep intimacy with the Spirit that seemed so present to me. They were deaf to the divine language of their own souls and cut off from the spiritual realm that Jesus had promised was close at hand.

3. **Guide Note:** **Discernment.** I had learned to look backward and recognize thin places that surrounded me at particular points on my life journey. Now I was beginning to seek out those places on my own rather than just occasionally falling into them. I put on love for the Spirit, responding to its movement in the face of the resistance I was encountering to the pilgrimage. Following the light resonating in my soul, I was gradually drawn to recognize holy longings, not just my own, in my response to the revolutionary twenty-first-century perspective of the universe.

Journal, March 25, 2008: **Revering the Spirit.** I joined a spiritual director's peer group that met monthly in Decatur, Georgia. We shared our experiences of the Holy as a deeply present, active force in healing, and we companioned each other in responding to its movement in our work with others. Following each session, I met with the group facilitator, sharing with her my frustrations with all the negative reactions to the pilgrimage and my feeling that my spiritual yearning was being choked.

She did not direct, advise, rescue, or try to fix my situation. Companioning me in these struggles, sometimes with leading questions, sometimes with a sympathetic ear, she guided me back to writing as a way of attending to the divine dimension. She helped me view my times of stagnation as creative invitations to deepen my understanding of the soul's light. Questions or criticism that before would have turned me back from mystical moments now pushed me deeper to a more authentic place in understanding them. Writing helped me break through my self-imposed limitations, refocusing and clarifying the mystical experiences in my life.

Journal, June 9, 2008: Responding to the Spirit. I perceived the Spirit stirring when I returned to Iona. Three more applications grew our group to ten, the number needed for the pilgrimage. Iona was just as I remembered. I quickly fell into the way of contemplation, slowing down to pay more attention to the Spirit's presence in all things.

The Abbey Gift Shop was the first place I went, hoping to reconnect with a friend I'd met there on my first trip to the island. Miraculously she was there, and remembered the talismans she'd helped me find on my first visit. This time she asked me to meet her the next day. As I joined her again in the gift shop, she pulled a stone from her pocket and said, "I've been thinking about you and want you to have this talisman I selected from

Iona Sound to bless your journey to and from the Island." I had rediscovered the thinness of this place.

Journal, June 12, 2008: **Walking in the Soul's Light.** As I meandered through a pottery shop, a local craftsman engaged me in conversation. My admiration for a unique wooden bowl that seemed almost plucked whole out of its tree encouraged him to tell me his own story of being "plucked" out of the world. For the next fifteen minutes I heard how his abiding passion to do something with his hands had led him away from a profitable career in sales to the shop here on the island.

His devotion to the passion resonating in his heart emblazoned the remainder of a quiet, rainy afternoon. Still struggling with my own doubts about the authenticity of my intuitions, I found an empty bench in an undisturbed corner behind the Abbey. As I reflected on his story of trusting his

GUIDE

heart, a ray of sunlight broke through the clouds, flooding the cold dampness with sudden warmth. A similar uncanny warmth infiltrated the Abbey's evening chill as I joined in the evening hymn:

You are called to tell the story, passing words of life along.
Then to blend your voice with others as you sing the sacred song.
Christ be known with all our singing, filling all with songs of love.

In that mystical moment, I heard—in some way beyond my sensory or intellectual apprehension of reality—a call to tell my story of discovering "words of life"—of finding a spiritual kingdom near at hand. I was drawn to recognize a holy mission, not just my own, in sharing my story of being led to this mystical wildness through the contemplative way I had learned to follow in this end-time.

TRUST THE WILDNESS

Journal, January 21, 2009: **Enduring a Dark Night.** I visited with a friend who was struggling with cancer. He had grown up believing in a distant, supernatural God who intervened at times to manage the universe. Now, facing serious surgery and chemotherapy, he was thirsty for an assurance of a holy presence accompanying him through this valley of the shadow of death that his beliefs could not provide. He resorted to what had worked at other times in his professional life, aggressively seeking his own answers, reaching out for more tests, more therapies, more specialists, desperately trying to control the uncontrollable.

Lamenting God's absence and doubting divine intervention, he did not know what to look for or how to look for it. Just when he needed to go deeper, his spiritual journey had come to a stop.

Journal, March 26, 2009: Cultivating Habits of the Heart. A memorial service for a physician who had served many summers at camp answered, for me, one question with which my friend was grappling: *how* to look. The gathering evolved into a testament to the formative influence of the camp experience on the physician's life and the lives of so many in attendance that day. I was struck anew at the intensity and enthusiasm with which they saw their camping experience as a vital component in shaping their character.

Reflecting on their witness later that evening, I awoke to the serendipitous similarities between camping and the practices I had learned at Columbia. Camping was by nature a contemplative experience. It epitomized a retreat from ordinary life. In one form or another, it provided time for a meditative thought, activities for practicing a principle or virtue, and an opportunity for reflection afterward. My camping years, I now saw, had been an annual immersion into contemplative ways, a retreat that had allowed me to cultivate the habits of the heart needed to delve deeper into the spiritual dimension of life.

Journal, July 21, 2009: **Embracing Oneness.** The answer to my friend's other question, *what* to look for, came to me later that spring at a retreat at Ghost Ranch in northern New Mexico. There, I was ushered into an awareness of the "oneness" of all life. New findings in mathematics, in biology, in physics, in ecology, and a host of other areas were reaffirming ancient spiritual teachings about the ultimate interconnectivity, the inextricable interdependence of all forms of life. New research was aligning with ancient wisdom about an energy that flows through the universe, connecting all living beings yet transcending any particular expression of life.

GUIDE

I became conscious of this mystical oneness during moments of solitude in the desert. As I sought the shade of an old bunkhouse in the heat of the morning, a northern junco regularly joined my space. A slate grey bird about the size of a sparrow, it was in no way out of the ordinary, but the dependability of the arrival of this bit of wildness during my time of reflection caught my attention.

In the intimate affinity that I developed with this small creature as we shared a moment of quiet, I became aware of something greater than both of us. I perceived our oneness as a natural wildness—an untamed breath of life that was part of each of us, connecting both of us to something greater than either of us. I realized that the boundaries between the wildness in the bird and the similar, though less obvious, wildness in me and the wild, spiritual cosmos were imagined. It was all part of a larger spiritual whole.

This wildness—creative energy—holy spirit—was flowing through both of us and through all life. While instinctive to the bird, this quiet all-encompassing immanent spiritual energy was less obvious to me, a postmodern individual heavily dependent on reason. Yet, during times of contemplation it became magnified by my soul, allowing me to hear and understand its mystical movement. My experience of this wild oneness that was within—yet transcendent of the present—was the presence of something *more* for which my friend was thirsty in his battle with cancer.

This new revelation empowered me to tell the story of my journey to the mystical kingdom through contemplative practices that led me to

GUIDE

hear and respond to the divine language of my
soul.

Journal, June 15, 2013: **Becoming a Guide.**
The result is the story you have just read. It is my
story of learning to trust the wildness—to walk the
way of contemplation, following the light of my
soul. I rejoice in its completion and hope it will
encourage you to become more mindful of the
unique gift of the Spirit reaching out in your life.
Daily worries and responsibilities weigh heavy on
the heart, distracting us from the deeper
movement of the Spirit. If this guide helps you
become more contemplative in your actions and
more trustful of a spiritual presence infusing this
end-time, I will have found my heart-path, the
place where the Holy is active in my life now.

*You...have put on the new self, which is being
renewed in knowledge in the image of its
Creator.* Colossians 3:10

TRUST THE WILDNESS

Ponder

1. Where are you in this end-time: leaving home, confronting a stop sign or a crossroad, struggling through a dark night, or making way?
2. What false forces lead you to resist being attentive to your soul?
3. What practices encourage you to be more mindful of your soul?
4. Who helps you see and name the experience of the Holy reaching out to you?
5. What new beginnings are drawing you?

■ ■

There is a divinity that shapes our ends,
rough-hew them how we will.
Hamlet, Act V, Scene II

CPSIA information can be obtained
at www.ICGtesting.com
Printed in the USA
FFOW01n1727101114
8692FF